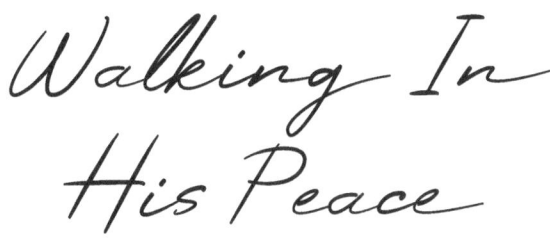

Walking In His Peace

A Daily Devotional

I0559509

Kimberly Moses

REJOICE
Essential Publishing

Walking In His Peace/Kimberly Moses

ISBN-13: 978-1-956775-97-6

Acknowledgments

This book idea was given to me years ago by the Lord. When God first told me to write, He instructed me to write a blog. Afterward, He told me to turn the blog into a book. After my first book was authored, God gave me a list of 21 books. I thought I was finished writing, but during devotion time with the Lord, He downloaded many more books, including this book about peace. God's timing is strategic because I had to press through to write even when spiritually attacked. Yet I stayed encouraged as I meditated and digested the Word of God concerning peace. This book is for those who are stressed and want to experience God's peace in the greatest capacity.

Table of Contents

Walking In His Peace

VIII

Introduction

Can you imagine constantly feeling like something terrible will happen to you? I felt that way every day for five years. I had anxiety, and the devil tormented me. The enemy told me that I was going to die every day and that he was going to kill me. I was stressed, and I did not have God's peace. I was afraid to leave my house. I couldn't enjoy the full life God promised me because I constantly looked over my shoulder.

You permit the enemy to wreak havoc whenever you are bound by sin. I did not get God's constant peace in my life until I repented for my sins and started to live right. Sin will push the presence of God out of your life, but a lifestyle of holiness will welcome the presence of God in your life.

Why? Because you will grieve the Holy Spirit when you constantly sin against Him. However, when you obey Him, you show God you love Him. How many people do you see drowning in addiction to drugs, committing suicide, sick, depressed, or living a defeated life? If you don't know anyone, go on social media and scroll. You will see many people struggling in those areas.

As children of the King, we should have God's peace. Our mission is to share our faith with others so they can experience God's peace for themselves. It's a wonderful feeling to feel God's refreshing presence every day. When I was bound in sin, God's presence was not in my life. However, when I got "saved for real," His presence came into my room during prayer, worship, or just spending time with Him. I finally experienced His peace.

Too many people are demonized and tormented by the devil just like I was, but Jesus came to set the captives free *(Luke 4:18-21)*. As God's children, we have the power of the Holy Spirit living inside us, and God anoints us to destroy the works of the kingdom of darkness (*Colossians 1:13, 1 John 3:8)*. I always tell people that peace is a gift. Many people in the world do not have God's peace. They are trying to fill a void that only God can fill. They are sleeping around, shopping, drinking, doing drugs, etc. When you walk uprightly before God, He will give you peace that surpasses all understanding, no matter what the enemy is trying to do to distract or derail you. As children of God, we think differently and don't let little things stress us out. We learn how to trust God throughout everything. My prayer is that God will give you peace throughout this book. At the end of each devotional is a prayer and a reflection to help you strategize maximizing God's peace in your life. I will share testimonies of circumstances where I was tested and tried, but God gave me peace.

Chapter 1

Importance of God's Peace

The Bible calls Jesus the prince of peace (Isaiah 9:6). Why? This verse is one of the prophecies of Isaiah. God has many names in this particular verse. However, this verse describes Jesus Christ, the Messiah, as the prince of peace. "Sar" is the Hebrew word for peace. Let's dig deeper; the purpose of the role of royalty is to rule over a territory. In this scriptural description, peace is described as Jesus Christ's territory. This verse indicates that Jesus Christ controls peace. Just think about it. No matter the enemy's agenda, Jesus Christ can control the situation. Have you ever received some devastating news, but when you prayed, suddenly, you had peace? That's because Jesus Christ is on the throne, and God is in control.

John 14:27 says, "Peace I leave with you, my peace I give unto you: not as the world giveth, give I unto you. Let not your heart be troubled, neither let it be afraid."

The scripture above reminds us that Jesus Christ gives us peace differently than the world. Worldly peace is temporary, but God's peace is everlasting. Jesus tells us that He has overcome the world and not to allow anything to stress us to the point where our hearts are troubled. The verse above is a great example of how our God is sovereign and supreme. He reigns. I have experienced some crazy circumstances, yet I can praise God that I maintained my sanity and I am not in a mental institution. Let's look at four aspects of what God's peace can do in our lives.

GOOD HEALTH

Stress can make you sick. You are not experiencing God's peace when you're stressed. Stress can make your hair grey out prematurely and cause panic or anxiety attacks. Now, I had my share of panic attacks, but since I have God's peace, those are a thing of the past. Stress is a silent killer. When some people are stressed out, they're not sleeping well. Sleep is vital for our health and well-being. God even rested on the seventh day. When God created Eve, He put Adam in a deep sleep and took one of Adam's ribs to form Eve (Genesis 2:22-24). When you're stressed, your appetite may be altered. Some people's stomachs get queasy. Some people overeat. They may resort to eating comfort foods such as a bucket of ice cream or fried chicken to cope with their emotions. These foods are great to consume in moderation, but ingesting too much can increase cholesterol and blood sugar, resulting in unhealthy pounds. When some people get stressed, they start to have an attitude problem and lash out at those close to them, such as their family members or friends. However, your attitude will be checked when you get in God's presence and spend time with Him. How can you get an attitude with those you supposedly love when you have God's peace, and you're walking in love?

When you're stressed, you have a burden on you.

Matthew 11:28 says, "Come to me, all you who are weary and burdened, and I will give you rest."

Notice the word "rest" in the scripture above. When you're resting, you feel great. You are in a mood of tranquility, and you are not worried about anything. We experience this when the Lord gives us rest. When we go to Him, we can *cast our cares upon Him because He cares for us (1 Peter*

5:7). We can trust God by giving Him the problem or circumstance. If you're feeling stressed about something, just say, "Lord, I give you this stressful situation, and I trust you to work it out because everything will work out for my good. I've been called according to your plans and purposes, and I love you."

The enemy wants us to stress ourselves out, leading us to die prematurely and not fulfill God's plans and purposes for our lives. Maybe you knew someone who, when they got stressed out, their blood pressure elevated, or they started having heart-related issues. The devil is a liar! God commands peace.

RIGHT MINDSET

Years ago, in my book, *Conquering The Mind: A Daily Devotional,* I shared my testimony in detail of how the Lord delivered me from anxiety. During those dark times, I did not have the peace of God. I noticed that when I had the right mindset and renewed my mind, I started experiencing the peace of God. During tribulations and trials, the first thing our flesh wants to do is to worry. However, we have to renew our minds every single day. When we get a bad report, we have to think about God's scriptures in our minds. When someone is trying to attack, persecute, speak evil of your well-doing, or slander you, you can have God's peace. You have developed a relationship with the Father, knowing He defends, provides, and cares for us. The enemy loves to attack our minds, but we can counterattack with the Sword of the Spirit *(Ephesians 6:17)*. God's word is sharper than a two-edged sword, and His word prevails. In other words, God's word has the final say and is the final judgment. If you struggle to think the right thoughts, I highly suggest you take time daily to meditate on the word of God. I have a book called, *"The Art Of Meditation: A Daily Devotional."* In that book, I share my testimony of how the Lord took me to another level and how I started to feel the presence of God as I had never before when I started meditating on the scriptures. With the right mindset, you won't allow your mind to entertain or dwell on negative outcomes. You will cast down every high thought or imagination that exalts itself against the knowledge of God *(2 Corinthians 10:5-7)*. You will not work yourself up but have God's peace.

HOPE

In Jesus Christ, we always have hope. But with God on our side, our situation is not hopeless. As a child of God, we can see the hand of God in every storm. When the disciples were on the ship, and the storm came that rocked the boat back and forth, Jesus Christ was with them. The disciples were afraid, and they woke up Jesus. He rebuked them for their lack of faith. He spoke to the wind and the waves, and they obeyed His voice. He said, "Peace be still, and know I am God." This passage of scripture is symbolic of our situation during trials and tribulations. We should always hope for the best. If God brought us to something, He will bring us through it. We are not alone. God says He will never leave us nor forsake us. We have to ask God for wisdom in the trials. We can have His peace because God will change our perspective. He will show us what we need to learn in any circumstance, and the trials will work out for our good.

Romans 15:13 (ESV) says, "May the God of hope fill you with all joy and peace in believing, so that by the power of the Holy Spirit you may abound in hope."

Our God is the God of all hope. When we have hope, our faith is strong, and we have godly character despite the storm we suffer. Look at the following scriptures. You will see how suffering produces the endurance that we need.

Romans 5:3-4 (ESV) says, "Not only so, but we also glory in our sufferings, because we know that suffering produces perseverance; 4 perseverance, character; and character, hope."

When we're walking in faith, we have peace. We aren't stressing about anything. There is no doubt when you're walking by faith.

Hebrews 11:1 says, "Now faith is the substance of things hoped for, the evidence of things not seen."

Faith is the substance of the things we hope for. Notice the word "Hope." When you're hoping for something, you are charging your faith to believe God for the miraculous. You have to guard your heart and know that in God's timing, everything will work out. Did you know that the opposite of hope is doubt, unbelief, faithlessness, or anxiety? These characteristics are not in someone who is walking in God's peace. Can you see how everything comes together when God's peace manifests in your life? Don't take the bait of being hopeless because you will set yourself up to be helpless, and that's what the devil wants. He doesn't want you to put your trust in God. He wants you to be ignorant that *God is a very present help in times of need and trouble (Psalm 46:1).*

BETTER RELATIONSHIPS

Peace is essential in relationships. The devil loves to stir up strife and division. He knows that there is strength in numbers. One can chase 1000, and two can put 10,000 to flight (Deuteronomy 32:30). We can accomplish great things together.

In Genesis 11, the people worked together to build a tower named Babel. However, their motives for building the tower weren't aligned with God's, so He had to intervene. Imagine what we could do if our motives were pleasing to God's sight.

We see much division and fighting throughout the body of Christ. Read the following scriptures carefully because our relationships matter.

Mark 3:25 says, "A house divided against itself cannot stand."

We are to be peacemakers. Even if you aren't wrong, it's all about being humble. Sometimes, the Holy Spirit will convict you to apologize. The Holy Spirit will direct you to be silent in a conflict.

Proverbs 17:28 says, "A fool is considered wise when he is silent."

We must renew our mindset and know that certain conversations are beneath us.

2 Timothy 2:24 says, "The Lord's servants must not be quarrelsome."

Romans 7:18 says, "The flesh produce no good thing."

Proverbs 16:7 says, "When a man's ways pleases the Lord, He will make even his enemies at peace with him."

We must recognize the devil that is in operation and get a strategy from Heaven on how to combat the powers of hell. *Exodus 14:14 tells us to keep our peace, and the Lord will fight for us.* Do you think you can defend yourself better than God can? So many of us do. When you have peace in your relationships, things go smoothly. We must follow God's word because we are called to *live peaceably with all men (Romans 12:18).* We shouldn't stir up drama or division. *Romans 16:17* warns us to stay away from such divisive people. Imagine having someone come to you full of mess and trouble. After the conversation ends, you feel weighed down, heavy, and stressed out. You aren't walking in peace anymore. You now have to get back in the presence of the Lord to dump all of the baggage that was just dumped on you to maintain peace and sanity.

The enemy causes strife in marriages. It is stressful working all day and coming home to a chaotic house. However, coming home after working all day to a house full of peace and love is a blessing. Our home should be our haven. The Bible is adamant about working things out with our brothers and sisters in Christ. Even if we have a gift we are offering at the altar, we need to leave that gift there and make things right with our brothers and sisters (Matthew 5:23-24). God has given us the *ministry of reconciliation (2 Corinthians 5:18).* The enemy wants to cause unforgiveness and offense where we can't even speak peaceably to one another. As a result, we end up harboring unforgiveness, bitterness, and pain inside our hearts, and we miss out on God's blessings. One example is in Genesis 37:4 with Joseph's brothers. The enemy set jealousy and hatred in their hearts, and they could not speak peaceably to Joseph. They took their eyes off of God and His purpose for their lives. Instead, they put their eyes on man and started comparing themselves to why their father (Jacob) favored their brother more than them. Don't take the enemy's bait by taking your eyes off God and putting them on man. God has a plan for each of us. He is calling us to make peace in our relationships. If you are jealous of someone, ask the Holy Spirit to remove it from your heart and help you love the person. Be happy when God is blessing them, and focus on walking in the things God has for your life.

Let's face it. We need God's peace. People are hurting, and they are looking for a Savior. Our job is to point people back to Jesus Christ and demonstrate God's peace. Don't be full of the devil, causing problems or tension everywhere you go. People are drawn to you when you have peace and want to be around you. God will give you counsel and wisdom. When you have God's peace, you can focus better and do what you're called to do more effectively. When you're stressed out, how can you finish the project efficiently? How can you fully enjoy all the blessings God has bestowed upon you when stressed out? When you're enjoying God's peace, you don't care about anything in this world because you know that things are out of your control and God has a plan. Even after an intense season of warfare, God will give you peace and a season of rest. Don't fret because God is working things out.

Day 1

Peace In the Land

Leviticus 26:6 says, "And I will give peace in the land, and ye shall lie down, and none shall make you afraid: and I will rid evil beasts out of the land, neither shall the sword go through your land."

There is so much going on in the nations. There are crimes of hatred. There are discrimination crimes. There are wars, and there are rumors of wars. There's hunger and famine. There are cyber-attacks. There is anger in the atmosphere. There's violence against the church. There's violence everywhere. There are murders, and the crime rate is at an all-time high. God promised us peace in our communities. When the Saints get together and pray and stand on the word of God, God can release peace in the land. We can lie down at night without feeling afraid. We don't have to lose sleep because God will protect us, regardless of what is going on in the world. We don't have to be afraid of bombings or threats against our society because God will guard our hearts and minds in peace. Even when our nation is under severe attack from a natural enemy, such as a nation that despises us, God will protect us. When there are vicious attacks against us, God will give us peace.

I remember one day going to Walmart, and a couple was fighting. They were cursing each other out, and the man roughed up the female. We were at the checkout line, and the couple was extremely loud. I was getting super annoyed and started praying in tongues under my breath. I bound up the enemy's attack because I did not want the fighting to escalate. I didn't know if the guy had a gun and would start shooting others. I took authority over the atmosphere in Jesus' name, and the situation immediately de-escalated. The couple finished checking out, and they left the store. As children of God, there may be situations that demand peace. We can release the peace of God in our environment. I'm grateful that no one was hurt that day because there are many attacks in grocery stores nationwide.

Dear Heavenly Father,

Thank you for giving us peace in the land. Lord, we thank you for protecting us from unseen dangers and de-escalating pending dangers before us. Thank you, Father, for loosing peace in the land. Thank you, Father, for your hedge of protection around us as we lay our heads down at night. Thank you, Father, for delivering us from the spirit of fear. Thank you, Lord, for keeping us as we obey your voice and follow your commands. Thank you, Lord, for protecting us from cyber-attacks, famine, and destruction that lay waste at noonday. We're so grateful for your peace in Jesus' name, amen.

REFLECTION:

During times of crisis, how can you be a peacemaker?

_____

_____

_____

_____

_____

_____

_____

_____

_____

_____

_____

_____

_____

_____

Day 2

The Lord Give You Peace

Numbers 6:24-26 says, "The Lord bless you and keep you; the Lord make his face shine on you and be gracious to you; the Lord turn his face toward you and give you peace."

The scripture above, known as the Aaronic Blessing, holds profound significance in spiritual warfare. Aaron, a Levite and one of the head priests was Moses' Prophet. This blessing, often given as a benediction or closing of worship or church services worldwide, is a powerful reminder of our need for God's Blessing. In a world where many seek to curse us, the Blessing of the Lord fortifies our lives.

In ministry, I never imagined that I would go through so much warfare. I constantly spent my days pouring out to others and serving them with the gifts that God placed on my life. However, not everyone is happy with what I am doing. Over time, I have met people operating in witchcraft or those who were sent from the enemy to try to curse me. Yet the Bible reminds me that I am blessed. No one can curse whom God has blessed. I have received all types of threats, but God gave me peace, and I was not afraid of the demonic threats. God will bless us and keep us from the demonic attack. He shines His glory upon us and gives us peace that surpasses all understanding.

Dear Heavenly Father,

Thank you for blessing me in all of my doing. Thank you for keeping me during the good times and the bad times. Thank you for thinking of me even when I felt discouraged or overwhelmed by the trials in this life. Thank you for being gracious to me and always showing up in my time of need. Thank you, Lord, for shining your countenance towards me. Thank you, Lord, for pouring out your glory upon my life. Your presence is a great comfort to me. You bring me joy, peace, strength, and hope to continue. In Jesus' name, I pray, amen.

REFLECTION:

Name a time when you felt God's peace during spiritual warfare. How did you overcome the attack?

_____

_____

_____

_____

_____

_____

_____

_____

_____

_____

_____

_____

_____

_____

_____

_____

_____

_____

_____

_____

_____

_____

_____

_____

_____

Day 3

I Will Lie Down In Peace

Psalm 4:8 says, "In peace I will lie down and sleep, for you alone, Lord, make me dwell in safety."

In the Psalm above, it is a reminder of God's peace. David wrote this psalm to remind people to meditate on God's ways. He's reminding people to believe in God's promises. David had the gift of writing and wrote many psalms. He understood the art of worship and meditation. He was known as a man after God's own heart. His writings touched the nation, leaving a legacy for generations to come. God will also use your writings to remind people to trust Him fully. David trusted God to protect him throughout his days.

I remember when I first got saved, and I was dealing with nightmare spirits almost every night. It was like the enemy took vengeance on me. I did not have God's peace throughout the night. I was afraid to go back to sleep because I could still feel an evil presence in my bedroom. Sometimes, as I opened my eyes, I saw dark shadows with red eyes standing over me. All I knew was to read the Bible and call on Jesus. During those times, when I flipped through the Bible, I learned how to pray against the demonic attack. Eventually, I started experiencing God's peace as I laid down at night because the enemy was defeated when I opened my mouth and prayed to my God.

Dear Heavenly Father,

Thank you for your peace throughout the night. Lord, keep us from the evil one. Lord, send angels to watch over us throughout the night. God, you watch over Israel, and you never sleep or slumber. I bind up the terror of the night; I bind up the nightmare spirit in the name of Jesus. I don't have to be afraid of the terror at night. According to Psalms 4:8, I decree that I will lie down in peace in Jesus's name. Amen.

REFLECTION:

What should you do when a nightmare spirit is harassing you?

_____

_____

_____

_____

_____

_____

_____

_____

_____

_____

_____

_____

_____

_____

_____

_____

_____

_____

_____

_____

Day 4

The Lord Blesses His People with Peace

Psalm 29:11 says, "The Lord gives strength to his people; the Lord blesses his people with peace."

As believers in Jesus Christ, we will endure trials and tribulations. Throughout scripture, we can read about God's people and see how the hand of the Lord moved as they cried out to Him. Psalms 29 is an excellent reminder that God's mighty voice breaks through Cedars, shakes the desert, and strips the forest bear. The voice of God amplifies above the craziest trials in life. If we can only hear the still, small voice of the Holy Spirit. This psalm reminds us that God would never leave or forsake us.

I remember going through financial challenges and learning to discern the voice of God. I had a good job. I had degrees but I was living paycheck to paycheck. I was late on many bills and faced eviction. I heard the Lord, and He told me not to worry about money and that I would never be homeless. I was stressed out. I wanted to cry, and I felt the weight of the world crushing me. But when I heard God's voice, I received peace. Miraculously, God honored His word, and I was not homeless. God blessed someone so they could bless me. They paid my rent for the rest of the year and moved me into a new apartment.

Dear Heavenly Father,

Thank you for blessing your people with peace. Lord, we would be in a mental asylum if it wasn't for your peace. Lord, your peace keeps us sane and keeps us from worrying about things that are out of our control. Your peace gives us the faith we need to keep holding on. Lord, bless us to hear your voice amid our struggles and tribulations. I decree that we will trust your word and hold onto your promises regardless of what it looks like. In Jesus' mighty name, we pray, amen.

REFLECTION:

Share a time when God made a promise, but it seemed like the opposite was happening. How did you keep yourself from doubting?

_____

_____

_____

_____

_____

_____

_____

_____

_____

_____

_____

_____

_____

_____

_____

_____

_____

_____

_____

_____

_____

_____

_____

Day 5

Seek Peace And Pursue It

Psalms 34:12-14 says, "Whoever of you loves life and desires to see many good days, keep your tongue from evil and your lips from telling lies. Turn from evil and do good; seek peace and pursue it."

The scriptures above are a great reminder to seek peace and pursue it. The enemy loves to creep in and cause strife and division. We are commanded to live in harmony. We are commanded to be peacemakers. Our flesh is naturally wicked. However, as children of God, we must yield this flesh in subjection to Jesus Christ. Gossiping and bickering may tempt us, but we must take the high road and seek peace. There will be people with different personalities, which we might not care for, but with God's help, we can learn to love people. Apostle Peter reminds the church, in First Peter chapter 3:8-12, to live in harmony, to seek peace and pursue it.

There are many scandals on social media, and many people go around causing discord. However, the Bible reminds us to keep our tongues from evil and our lips from telling lies. We must turn from evil to do good, seek peace, and pursue it. I have had people write nasty blogs about me and falsely accuse me for righteousness' sake. But I chose to seek peace and not give into my flesh, where I act out of character. I decided to love, and I prayed for my enemies. God bless me despite the vicious lies and attacks against my ministry or character. The lies against me fell to the ground, exposing the person the enemy was using. When you see God's peace in every situation, God will vindicate you.

Dear Heavenly Father,

When my enemies are surrounding me, keep me, Lord. Let me be a peacemaker, Father. Let me pursue your peace instead of drama. Bless me to always turn from evil and do the right thing in thy sight. Lord, help my mouth to speak words of edification. I shun evil from coming out of my mouth in Jesus' name. Help me, Lord, to love people and to live in harmony with others. In Jesus's mighty name, I pray. Amen.

REFLECTION:

What should believers do when there is a scandal on social media?

_____

_____

_____

_____

_____

_____

_____

_____

_____

_____

_____

_____

_____

_____

_____

_____

_____

_____

_____

_____

Day 6

The Meek Will Enjoy Peace & Prosperity

Psalm 37:10-11 says, "A little while, and the wicked will be no more; though you look for them, they will not be found. But the meek will inherit the land and enjoy peace and prosperity."

The scriptures above remind us not to get jealous when seeing the wicked prosper. The wicked are seeking peace in temporary things such as drugs, alcohol, wealth, fame, etc.; however, true peace comes from God. His peace is everlasting. The wicked are trying to gain the whole world but losing their souls. On the contrary, the righteous have God's peace, and with God's help, they inherit the land.

When you seek God's Kingdom of righteousness, everything else will be added, such as your heart's desires.

I learned that when I live rightly before God, I live in constant peace. I may not have everything I want, but I have everything I need. God longs to bless me. He gives me the desires of my heart in His timing. He touches our hands to prosper when we are in His will. When I sought God for income, He gave me a business idea: to open a publishing company. He made sure to bless it and to send a steady stream of clientele. Over time, I turned down projects I knew grieved the Holy Ghost and those I had no peace about. As a result, I have felt God's peace on the projects that had His stamp of approval, and He blessed me in completing them.

Dear Heavenly Father,

We are deeply grateful for Your reminder that the meek will enjoy Your peace and prosper in Jesus' name. We thank You for prospering the works of our hands. Most of all, we thank You, God, for sending Your only begotten Son, Jesus, so that whoever believes in Him will not perish but have everlasting life. We are truly blessed to experience Your peace due to living uprightly before You. In Jesus' mighty name, we pray. Amen.

REFLECTION:

What can we do when we are tempted to feel that the wicked are more prosperous than we are?

_____

_____

_____

_____

_____

_____

_____

_____

_____

_____

_____

_____

_____

_____

_____

_____

_____

_____

_____

_____

_____

_____

_____

_____

Day 7

Righteousness and Peace

Psalm 85:10 says, "Love and faithfulness meet together; righteousness and peace kiss each other."

In the Psalm above, we see beautiful imagery. God is love, and His disciples love one another. We develop faithfulness when we allow the Holy Spirit to do a work in our lives. Also, through Christ Jesus, we are the righteousness of God. The righteous seek God's peace. They don't like drama, strife, or division. Peace and righteousness kiss each other. The connection between righteousness and peace is very intimate. We see through Christ's life on earth and His ministry, He was a peacemaker. In Matthew 26, during the night, when the mob captured Jesus. , Peter cut off the soldier's ear. Jesus stretched out his hand and restored the soldier's ear. He told Peter if you live by the sword, you will die by the sword. Jesus is the ultimate peacemaker.

Growing up, I fought almost every week. My family raised me to fight. My mother and aunts fought. My family even told me that if I did not win the fight when I got home, I would get my butt whooped. I learned to trust God to fight my battles when I got saved and didn't want to take matters into my own hands anymore. I decided to be a peacemaker because the *Lord's servants must not be quarrelsome (2 Timothy 2:24).* I didn't want to give the enemy room to operate in my life.

Dear Heavenly Father,

We thank you for your word. Your word is true, and you sanctify us in truth; your word prevails. Thank you for changing me from the inside out as I experience your presence. I don't want to grieve your Holy Spirit. Lord, bless me to take on Christ's like characteristics as I spend time in your presence. In Jesus' mighty name, I pray. Amen.

REFLECTION:

What is the best way to handle conflict during a disagreement?

_____

_____

_____

_____

_____

_____

_____

_____

_____

_____

_____

_____

_____

_____

_____

_____

_____

_____

_____

_____

_____

_____

_____

Day 8

Peace For Those Who Love God's Law

Psalm 119:165 says, "Great peace have those who love your law, and nothing can make them stumble."

Psalms 119 is one of the longest Psalms in the Bible. God will bless you with great peace when you love Him and His law. You won't stumble because you aren't stressing out or wavering to the left or the right. You aren't walking in doubt or unbelief. You have peace because you trust God's promises, regardless of how you feel or how impossible it may look. You are walking by faith and not by sight. You love God, and you have developed a relationship with Him.

You have history with God, so if God did it before, He can do it again.

I often had deadlines and needed God to move right then and there. I went to the Father, and I petitioned Him. Suddenly, an overmounting peace came upon me, and I knew deep down that everything would be OK. Even though it seemed like the odds were stacked against me, God always made a way. I decided to trust God with everything within me because I know He sees my heart and knows my thoughts, and I don't want to let Him down. Even when people around me told me it would never work out, and they doubted what God would do in my life, God proved them wrong. God knows those who trust in Him. As a result, God kept His word, and I received a breakthrough.

Dear Heavenly Father,

Thank you for your word. Help me to put your word in my heart so I don't sin against you. Lord, bless me to love your word so my heart and mind can be shielded with your peace. Thank you, God, for reminding me of your word daily because it keeps me from stumbling. Your word keeps me on a straight, narrow path. Lord, you can't lie. I know you will do everything that you promised me. So why should I worry? Thank you for answering this prayer in Jesus' mighty name. Amen.

REFLECTION:

Reflect on a time when God met your deadline. What emotions did you feel? Do you believe that God will bless you like that again?

_____

_____

_____

_____

_____

_____

_____

_____

_____

_____

_____

_____

_____

_____

_____

_____

_____

_____

_____

_____

_____

_____

_____

Day 9

Those Who Promote Peace Have Joy

Proverbs 12:20 says, "Deceit is in the hearts of those who plot evil, but those who promote peace have joy."

The devil is a deceiver, using people he deceives to do evil. Their hearts are far from God, and they plot evil. They don't have peace. They get joy and satisfaction from seeing others' demise. However, those who promote peace and live upright before God have supernatural joy. Because in God's presence is the fullness of joy. God will ensure that you have constant peace and that you are not tormented by the evil one. The enemy torments those who do wicked. They seek things to find peace in sex, drama, chasing wealth, fame, etc.

Over time, God blessed me with the wisdom to set boundaries. You teach people how to treat you. For instance, this lady came to me and tried to gossip about our Pastor. I didn't give her the response she was hoping for. Instead, I said, "Did you pray for him?" My response shocked the lady because she wanted me to gossip with her. The next time the same lady came into my inbox trying to gossip about someone else, I didn't respond. That taught that lady to stay out of my inbox with drama. Eventually, she stopped trying to gossip with me about others. I decided to guard the peace of God in my life and not allow anything to weigh me down so I could experience His joy.

Dear Heavenly Father,

I am grateful for the supernatural joy You have bestowed on me. I humbly ask for Your blessings to establish healthy boundaries in my life and the courage to do what is right. I ask for Your protection over my heart and mind and Your guidance to remind those around me to pray and seek Your face. I ask for Your blessings to walk in love and set a positive example. I pray that You always keep me abiding in Your word. In Jesus' name, amen.

REFLECTION:

What are some ways where you have established healthy boundaries in your life?

_____

_____

_____

_____

_____

_____

_____

_____

_____

_____

_____

_____

_____

_____

_____

_____

_____

_____

_____

_____

_____

_____

_____

Day 10

The Lord Causes Peace

Proverbs 16:7 says, "When the Lord takes pleasure in anyone's way, he causes their enemies to make peace with them."

This scripture is a powerful testament to the fact that when your ways please the Lord, He will not only make your enemies at peace with you but also defend you against them. Throughout scripture, we witness the Israelites facing numerous adversaries. Yet, the Lord defended them and deterred their enemies from attacking them. God's protection is not just a shield but a force that instills fear in our enemies, making them think twice about raising a hand against His children. He even intervenes, speaking to our enemies and commanding them to leave us alone.

I remember that, in school, I had a lot of pride and went out of my way to defend myself. I would over-talk others to get my point across. When I started working in the hospital, I had to learn to depend on God to vindicate me. I had some people that did not like me. Yet they left me alone because I serve the Lord. Their efforts to get me fired backfired because I kept my mouth shut, didn't argue, or took matters into my own hands. Their efforts to slander my name did not work. Instead, God continued to bless and prosper me despite some of my co-worker's attempts to get me fired.

Dear Heavenly Father,

Thank you for protecting my life, family, and ministry. I repent of all my sins and pray that I am pleasing in your sight. Lord, bless my way to please you so you can cause my enemy to be at peace with me. Keep me humble and gentle. Thank you for shielding me against demonic attacks. Thank you, Lord, for placing a wall of fire around me and all my assets. In Jesus' mighty name, I pray. Amen.

REFLECTION:

What should we do when an enemy is coming against us? How can we handle this situation in a godly manner?

_____

_____

_____

_____

_____

_____

_____

_____

_____

_____

_____

_____

_____

_____

_____

_____

_____

_____

_____

_____

_____

_____

Day 11

Keep Yourself In Perfect Peace

Isaiah 26:3-4 says, "You will keep in perfect peace those whose minds are steadfast, because they trust in you. Trust in the Lord forever, for the Lord, the Lord himself, is the Rock eternal."

The scriptures above are a great reminder to focus on Jesus for perfect peace. People put their peace on temporary things, but only Christ's peace is eternal and everlasting. Isaiah reminds us that God is our rock and His love is never-ending or never-changing. God is dependable and faithful. He won't let us down when we put our trust in Him. It's easy to focus on other things that will stress us out and cause us to doubt God's promises, but we have to renew our minds daily and put them back on Christ.

When I had anxiety for five years, meditating on Isaiah 26:3 kept me from having panic attacks. I remember walking down the hallways at work, passing my co-workers, and I wanted to start having a panic attack. But the scripture came into my mind, and I began to think about Jesus Christ. Immediately, the fear that was trying to come against me left, and I started to experience God's peace. The Lord began to minister to me and reminded me that I was not in harm's way and that there was nothing to fear. Over time, I remember this verse during stressful situations because Jesus is my source of peace.

Dear Heavenly Father,

Thank you for your peace that surpasses all understanding. Lord, I won't worry about how things will work out. Instead, I'm going to keep my mind on you. I will praise and thank you in advance before I see the promise. I know with you, Father, I have the victory. With you on my side, I will overcome these trials and tribulations. Thank you for helping me renew my mind in Jesus' mighty name. Amen.

REFLECTION:

What should we do when we are afraid?

_____

_____

_____

_____

_____

_____

_____

_____

_____

_____

_____

_____

_____

_____

_____

_____

_____

_____

_____

_____

_____

_____

_____

Day 12

No Peace For The Wicked

Isaiah 48:22 says, "There is no peace," says the Lord, "for the wicked."

This verse tells us there is no peace for the wicked. Some people use this verse to say there's no rest for the wicked. When you do evil things, you will reap what you sow. You may get away with it today, but it could catch up with you tomorrow, a year from now, or a decade. God is not mocked. Whatever someone sows, they are going to reap. No one truly gets away with anything. The wicked are constantly looking over their shoulders. They feel like something terrible is going to happen to them. The reason is that they have the devil running rampant in their life. The devil carries fear and torment. However, God's presence carries peace.

I remember being in the club scene and meeting many devil-bound people, and I was one of them. I had no peace, and the people around me did not either. This young lady who I was hanging out with would drink herself sick. She would vomit and pass out. When I looked her in her eyes, all I saw was darkness. I wasn't living right then, but I could still see darkness on her. Looking in the mirror at my own eyes, I saw the same darkness. I used to shake because the devil tormented me. I used to hear the devil speaking to me, telling me all kinds of evil things to do to myself. I had no peace until one day, I repented of my sins, and I surrendered my life to Christ. It has been a journey, but I refuse to go down that dark road.

Dear Heavenly Father,

Thank you for your peace. Draw me close to you and set me free. Thank you for sending your son Jesus to transform me from darkness unto your marvelous light. Deliver this wicked heart and help me do the right thing. Lord, help me to be surrounded by people who love you and those who will encourage me to do the right thing. Bad company corrupts good morals. I love you and want to know you in Jesus' mighty name. Amen.

REFLECTION:

Why don't the wicked have God's peace?

_____

_____

_____

_____

_____

_____

_____

_____

_____

_____

_____

_____

_____

_____

_____

_____

_____

_____

_____

_____

_____

_____

_____

_____

_____

Day 13

Blessed Are the Peacemakers

Matthew 5:9 says, "Blessed are the peacemakers, for they will be called children of God."

Peacemakers choose to take the high road. Instead of allowing the flesh to dominate them, they swallow any pride, and they decide to make peace. God has given them wisdom to handle conflicts and bless them with a godly resolution. With God's strength, they won't take the bait of the enemy and sin. They will think about the words coming out of their mouths because a soft answer turns away wrath. They will be reminded of various scriptures, *quick to hear, slow to speak (James 1:19), be angry but sin not*

(Ephesians 4:26-27), and that the *Lord's servants must not be quarrelsome (2 Timothy 2:24).*

You must be a peacemaker in a customer service job or working around people with different personalities. Sometimes, people can take their frustration out on you, and it's not your fault. Sometimes, our flesh wants to lash out and put the person in their place, but how can we win someone to Christ when we are allowing the devil to get us in our flesh? The flesh profits no good thing. We never know who's looking or whose lives we will impact, so being a peacemaker is the ultimate way to win souls for Jesus Christ. Once the onlookers or the person who had an attitude with us see how we handled the situation, they may repent and want to serve the God we serve.

Dear Heavenly Father,

Help me be a peacemaker. Lord, give me wisdom to work through friction, opposition, and relational challenges. Help my mouth not to speak words that will stir up wrath. Help me, God, not to walk in offense or pride. Help me, God, to be spirit-led, patient, gentle, and kind. Thank you for answering this prayer in Jesus' name. Amen.

REFLECTION:

How can you maintain peace when working in a stress-ful environment?

_____

_____

_____

_____

_____

_____

_____

_____

_____

_____

_____

_____

_____

_____

_____

_____

_____

_____

_____

_____

_____

_____

_____

_____

Day 14

Peace I Leave With You

John 14:27 says, "Peace I leave with you; my peace I give you. I do not give to you as the world gives. Do not let your hearts be troubled and do not be afraid."

There are so many things that are coming at us every day. If it's not one thing, it's another thing. That's life. But we're not alone because God said He will never leave or forsake us. It is so easy to lose sleep or your appetite because of stress. Worrying about things that are out of our control is so easy. You can have supernatural peace if you can renew your mind and bind up the spirit of fear. Decide to guard your heart, and don't allow any room to be anxious about anything.

My past was filled with pessimism and a constant fear of the worst. I couldn't see the positives in any situation, and my words were tainted with doubt and unbelief. Only when I fully surrendered to Christ Jesus did a profound shift occur. I recognized the deep-rooted fear within me and the need for significant deliverance. The Holy Spirit provided me with strategies to combat anxiety and maintain my peace. I now refuse to let my heart be troubled, knowing that Jesus Christ has already overcome the world.

Dear Heavenly Father,

Thank you for your peace and your hedge of protection around me. Thank you for delivering when I cry out to you. You are my strength and the anchor of my soul. I may not understand why I had to go through it now, but I will later. You work all things out for my good. Lord, give me an extra measure of faith to keep pressing on and not quit. I will wage a good warfare with my prophecies in Jesus' name. Amen.

REFLECTION:

What are the steps to wage a good warfare with your prophecies?

_____

_____

_____

_____

_____

_____

_____

_____

_____

_____

_____

_____

_____

_____

_____

_____

_____

_____

_____

Day 15

In Me, You May Have Peace

John 16:33 says, "I have told you these things, so that in me you may have peace. In this world, you will have trouble. But take heart! I have overcome the world."

Jesus Christ is the prince of peace and promised us He had overcome the world. The Bible talks about storms, trials, and tribulations. Looking through the scriptures, you will see that many people underwent various trials. Yet God was there when the people called out to Him, and He always moved miraculously. We can look to Jesus Christ, the author and perfecter of our faith, who has conquered this world whenever we go through something to get supernatural peace. We can put hope in him to break through. We can draw strength from Jesus Christ so we do not lose our minds during a trial. The word of God will prevail, and God's promises will surely come to pass.

When I first got saved, I was so naïve I thought Christians didn't have to go through trials and tribulations. That was far from the truth. Because I am a Christian, I started going through trials and tribulations. I got persecuted for my faith because I'm a woman in ministry. There is a saying that the devil doesn't mess with "nobodys." I also heard the phrase, "God gives the toughest battles to His strongest soldiers." Those two statements encouraged me not to quit the good fight of faith. The more trials I went through, the more I drew closer to God and discovered my purpose in Him. All things work out for our good because we love God and have been called according to His plans and purposes. We will go through things in life, but our rock is in Jesus Christ. He is the anchor of our souls.

Dear Heavenly Father,

Thank you for your peace while I endure various trials and tribulations. I am so grateful that Jesus Christ keeps me rooted and grounded in Him. Thank you, Lord, for blessing me not to lose my mind through all the things that I have endured. Thank you for sending encouraging words through your servants so I can keep holding on to the hem of Jesus' garments. Thank you for never leaving me nor forsaking me in Jesus Christ. Amen.

REFLECTION:

What is a powerful phrase or message that encouraged you during a trial?

_____

_____

_____

_____

_____

_____

_____

_____

_____

_____

_____

_____

_____

_____

_____

_____

_____

_____

_____

_____

Day 16

Life and Peace: Governed By the Spirit

Romans 8:6 says, "The mind governed by the flesh is death, but the mind governed by the Spirit is life and peace."

Whenever we allow positive thoughts to fill our minds, they bring hope and encouragement. This experience starkly contrasts the stress and torment that negative thoughts can bring, allowing the enemy to gain a foothold. When our mindset is carnal (flesh), it becomes a hostile environment for God (Roman 8). It's riddled with doubt, unbelief, fear, etc., leaving little room for faith. Remember, without faith, it is impossible to please God, and you miss a divine opportunity for God to show up powerfully in your life.

When I first started hearing the voice of God, He spoke many promises that seemed so far out of reach. Initially, I wanted to doubt what I heard because I was caught up in current circumstances and looking at all the odds stacked against me. I was overwhelmed by figuring out how God would do what He said. It's not our job to figure out how God will do it, but our job is to believe. I had to learn how to renew my mind by rebuking thoughts of doubt and repeating the prophecy out loud. I started to thank God in advance for the blessing. Eventually, God's word manifested. Some words happened immediately, while others happened several years later.

Dear Heavenly Father,

I pray that my thoughts are pleasing in your sight. I don't want a negative mindset that is hostile towards you. I want to be transformed by renewing my mind, and I will yield myself to your Spirit. Please help me to experience your peace, joy, and other fruits of the Holy Spirit daily. I bind up being led by my flesh. I don't want to do things with my strength or rely on self-produced resources. I don't want to walk down a path of destruction. I trust in you, God, as my source; everything else is just a resource in Jesus' name. Amen.

REFLECTION:

Write down one positive affirmation that you can confess today.

_____

_____

_____

_____

_____

_____

_____

_____

_____

_____

_____

_____

_____

_____

_____

_____

_____

_____

_____

_____

_____

_____

_____

_____

Day 17

Live At Peace With Everyone

Romans 12:17-18 says, "Do not repay anyone evil for evil. Be careful to do what is right in the eyes of everyone. If it is possible, as far as it depends on you, live at peace with everyone."

In society, people may think you are weak if you don't respond or say something to the person who may be talking junk about you. The enemy uses the person to slander your name and ruin your reputation. Preachers are bashing other preachers. The members of a congregation need to speak better of their leadership. The tension is at an all-time high in many circles. We don't have to prove a point because

God is our vindicator and defender. We should remember we are blessed when people speak evil of us or persecute us for righteousness' sake.

I used to be discouraged because I wanted to be liked by others and be in the crowd. No matter how hard I tried, I didn't fit in. I always tried to mind my business, but somehow, someone needed help. I went to the scriptures and saw in *Luke 6:26, "Woe to you when everyone speaks well of you."* In other words, not everyone will like us if we are in the will of God. If everyone speaks well of us, we may be doing something wrong. The false prophets (Hananiah) in the scriptures were popular, and contrarily, the real prophets (Jeremiah) were hated and feared (Jeremiah 28). No matter what someone says or does against you, keep your peace. God will fight for you.

Dear Heavenly Father,

I realize that only some will like me or be happy with what I do for you. I don't want to be in the in-crowd if it's going to cause me to grieve your spirit. If someone has a problem with me, I will do my best to make peace and to keep my heart pure. I want to obey you, God, even amid conflict. I decree that I will make peace regardless because I won't hold onto grudges, and you have given me the ministry of reconciliation. Thank you for answering this prayer in Jesus' name. Amen.

REFLECTION:

How can you make peace with those who may not like you?

_____

_____

_____

_____

_____

_____

_____

_____

_____

_____

_____

_____

_____

_____

_____

_____

_____

_____

_____

_____

_____

Day 18

Do What Leads to Peace

Romans 14:19 says, "Let us therefore make every effort to do what leads to peace and mutual edification."

In the Body of Christ, not everyone agrees on everything. For instance, some don't believe in women preachers. Others don't believe in women wearing pants. Some may not believe in the fivefold ministry, while some churches do. Lastly, some believers may not believe in eating certain foods. However, Apostle Paul reminds Christians to work hard at living at peace with others because we all should believe in Jesus and focus on winning souls for His kingdom. Some things dividing us are trivial, but we must be concerned with God's business.

Notice the words mutual edification in the above scripture. Some translations say mutual upbuilding. Our goal should be building others in the Body of Christ. We should not judge others because they are babes in the faith; we all have a process to go through. God will transform them more into His image as He did with us, the more mature saints. Our job is to love and to make peace. When I first got saved, I had self-righteous behavior, but over time, God humbled me and reminded me where He brought me from.

Dear Heavenly Father,

Thank you for your love and encouragement. If I have any unrighteous and self-righteous behavior, deliver me. I don't want to shake anyone's faith in you or cause someone to sin. Please help me to take the high road during the conflict. I decree that I will live peacefully with others and speak life to those around me. Bless me to stay in your will. Thank you for answering this prayer in Jesus' name. Amen.

REFLECTION:
How should you pray for a babe in Christ?

_____

_____

_____

_____

Day 19

May The Lord Fill You With Joy and Peace

Romans 15:13 says, "May the God of hope fill you with all joy and peace as you trust in him, so that you may overflow with hope by the power of the Holy Spirit."

Apostle Paul blessed the Roman church before He left. He prayed for their joy and peace. He reminds the church to trust in Jesus to experience an overflow of hope, joy, and peace in His presence. Apostle Paul shows us the importance of blessing a ministry and interceding for it when one departs from the church or when one's assignment is up. We should always strive to bless God's house and pray instead of leaving destructively.

Consider the case of an individual who once operated in a snake spirit in my ministry. They announced their departure, sowing seeds of discord. However, I took a different approach. I pulled the individual aside, encouraged them to leave silently, and blessed them. This incident underscores the importance of learning how to leave a ministry correctly. When I decided to leave a ministry, I sought a blessing from the leader, approaching them in humility and expressing what I felt led to do. I refrained from causing a scene or trying to dissuade others from joining that particular ministry.

Dear Heavenly Father,

Let me be planted in the house of the Lord. If it's time to leave a ministry, allow me to do so peacefully. I don't want to cause discord or stifle anyone's spiritual growth. I don't want to plant negative seeds about a leader in the people's minds. If I have any concerns about the church, I will bring them to you in prayer. I will obey if you instruct me to meet with the church leaders. Help me to walk in wisdom and do things with integrity in Jesus' name. Amen.

REFLECTION:
How should one leave a ministry or church peacefully?

Day 20

The Fruit of the Spirit Is Peace

Galatians 5:22-23 says, "But the fruit of the Spirit is love, joy, peace, forbearance, kindness, goodness, faithfulness, gentleness and self-control. Against such things there is no law."

We need the fruits of the Spirit in this Christian walk: love, joy, peace, forbearance, kindness, goodness, faithfulness, gentleness, and self-control. We have to die to self or kill the flesh because we must be Spirit-led. The flesh is the soulish realm, fighting against God's Spirit. The flesh wants to do everything against God. The works of the flesh are adultery, fornication, uncleanness, lasciviousness, idolatry, witchcraft, hatred, variance, emulations, wrath, strife, seditions, heresies, envyings, murders, drunkenness, and revellings. However, when we allow the Holy Spirit to develop the fruits of the Spirit within us, we are transformed. A notable change in our behavior, thoughts, and lifestyle will occur.

Before I became saved, flesh dominated me. I didn't love anyone except myself. I was very selfish and had an attitude problem. I was attracted to drama and enjoyed seeing street fights or people at their worst. I would spread gossip and turn people against each other. But God had a plan for my life. After a near-death encounter when I got in a car accident, I knew God was real. I decided to give Him a try. Eventually, I got saved, baptized, and filled with the Holy Spirit, and I allowed Him to birth the fruits of the Spirit in my life. I'm now a new creature in Christ, and the old man has passed away.

Dear Heavenly Father,

Please help me to be led by your Spirit. I know my flesh is displeasing to you. Help me live a consecrated lifestyle so I can bring this flesh under your subjection. I decree and declare that I will develop love, joy, peace, forbearance, kindness, goodness, faithfulness, gentleness, and self-control. I will not operate in the works of the flesh. Thank you for answering this prayer in Jesus' name. Amen.

REFLECTION:

How can we develop the fruits of the Spirit in our lives?

_____

_____

_____

_____

_____

_____

_____

_____

_____

_____

_____

_____

_____

_____

_____

_____

_____

_____

_____

Day 21

Destroying the Dividing Wall of Hostility

Ephesians 2:14-18 says, "For he himself is our peace, who has made the two groups one and has destroyed the barrier, the dividing wall of hostility, by setting aside in his flesh the law with its commands and regulations. His purpose was to create in himself one new humanity out of the two, thus making peace, and in one body to reconcile both of them to God through the cross, by which he put to death their hostility. He came and preached peace to you who were far away and peace to those who were near. For through him we both have access to the Father by one Spirit.'"

Throughout scripture, there have been divisions, such as the Jews and Gentiles. The Jews didn't want to associate with any other groups. When Jesus came, He broke down cultural barriers. He told the centurion soldier (a Gentile) that he had great faith (Matthew 8:10). In John 4, Jesus ministered to the Samaritan woman, and his disciples felt she wasn't significant enough to be taught. However, her testimony caused other Samaritans to come to see Jesus minister, and Jesus stayed in Samaria for three days, bringing people into the kingdom of God. Many people didn't understand why He would do these things. He demonstrated God's love for everyone, not just a particular race or religion. God doesn't want any of us to perish.

When God's Spirit is moving, racial and socioeconomic barriers are crossed. God desires unity, and He can bring different cultures together. During the Jim Crow era in the early 1900s, there was a black man named William Seymour. He wanted God and went to Bible College. However, he wasn't allowed to learn with all the other white students. He had to sit outside the school on the steps with a brown bag over his head. God saw his faithfulness and sacrifice and used this man to host the Azusa Street revivals. Blacks and whites came together peacefully to worship and experience the presence of God.

Dear Heavenly Father,

I am grateful for your work in breaking down the walls of hostility in our nations and showing us how to break down barriers in our community. I commit myself to loving everyone regardless of race, culture, or background. I ask for your guidance in winning souls for your kingdom and demonstrating your power on earth. I pray for a compassionate heart to draw people to you in Jesus' name. Amen.

REFLECTION:

How can you make peace with others with different beliefs or backgrounds?

_____

_____

_____

_____

_____

_____

_____

_____

_____

_____

_____

_____

_____

_____

_____

_____

_____

_____

_____

_____

_____

_____

_____

_____

_____

_____

_____

_____

_____

_____

_____

_____

_____

_____

_____

_____

_____

_____

_____

Day 22

Keeping Unity Through The Bond of Peace

Ephesians 4:2-6 says, "Be completely humble and gentle; be patient, bearing with one another in love. Make every effort to keep the unity of the Spirit through the bond of peace. There is one body and one Spirit, just as you were called to one hope when you were called; one Lord, one faith, one baptism; one God and Father of all, who is over all and through all and in all."

Before Jesus ascended on high, He prayed for His followers (John 17). He wanted unity among His believers because He knew that the devil would try to divide the church. The enemy specializes in division, and he knows that the church is stronger together. Imagine what the church can do in the world when we work together, lifting up the name of Jesus. Our communities, schools, businesses, and other major areas will be full of God's Spirit to bring change. Jesus warned us that a house divided against itself can not stand (Matthew 12:22-28). The church must be united.

Many times, the church fights over minor doctrinal differences. I used to tell people they were going to hell and be harsh with them because they weren't baptized in the name of Jesus. These people were baptized in the name of the Father, Son, and Holy Ghost. They loved God and were saved, but I came against them in my zeal. Over time, as I matured, I saw the error in my ways. Instead of focusing on another's salvation, I need to focus on working out my salvation in fear and trembling of the Lord and go out into the world and reach the lost souls. I let go of any need to argue and started loving people. As a result, the anointing on my life increased, and God began to trust me with more responsibility.

Dear Heavenly Father,

Help the church maintain unity through the bond of peace. Bless us to love each other in the church and reconcile our differences. You look at the heart and not the flesh.

Take any pride and selfish ambition out of my heart. Order my steps and create in me a pure heart. Bless me to walk in forgiveness. Thank you for answering this prayer in Jesus' name. Amen.

REFLECTION:

How can different churches come together?

_____

_____

_____

_____

_____

_____

_____

_____

_____

_____

_____

_____

_____

_____

_____

_____

_____

_____

_____

_____

_____

Day 23

The Peace of God will Guard Your Heart

Philippians 4:6-7 says, "Do not be anxious about anything, but in every situation, by prayer and petition, with thanksgiving, present your requests to God. And the peace of God, which transcends all understanding, will guard your hearts and your minds in Christ Jesus."

God commands us not to be anxious about anything. Trials will come, but God is a way-maker, and if we trust Him, we will come out victorious. Apostle Paul wrote the scriptures above to the Philippian church. He had a Damascus road encounter, and he went from killing Christians to becoming one. God used him to do great exploits. As he went to preach the gospel, many perse-cuted, beat, stoned, and imprisoned him. He was even shipwrecked and close to losing his life. Yet, the Holy Spirit instructed Paul to write these verses, reminding us not to worry because everything will work out for our good.

When I was overwhelmed with anxiety attacks, I would meditate on Philippians 4:6-7 and experience God's peace. God called me to preach His word, but my life was falling apart. I was going through a divorce, living paycheck to paycheck, hungry, on probation, and depressed. I couldn't see anything good coming out of my circumstances. Yet God used my wilderness experience and trials to give me a purpose and hope. I was able to write twenty-one books within a few years because God kept my mind and heart on Him. After that assignment was over, God gave me more books to write.

Dear Heavenly Father,

Thank you for guarding my heart and mind to stay on you. When I focus on your Son Jesus, I will receive peace that surpasses all understanding. The enemy may try to form attacks against me, but it will not prosper. No matter what, God, you are with me, and I'm an overcomer through you. I will no longer worry, but my faith is in you.

I decree that I will do great exploits. Thank you in advance for working everything out in Jesus' name. Amen.

REFLECTION:

Write down one testimony that God gave you. What steps did you take to go from having a test to a testimony?

_____

_____

_____

_____

_____

_____

_____

_____

_____

_____

_____

_____

_____

_____

_____

_____

_____

_____

_____

Day 24

Let Christ's Peace Rule In Your Hearts

Colossians 3:12-15 says, "Therefore, as God's chosen people, holy and dearly loved, clothe yourselves with compassion, kindness, humility, gentleness and patience. Bear with each other and forgive one another if any of you has a grievance against someone. Forgive as the Lord forgave you. And over these virtues put on love, which binds them all together in perfect unity. Let the peace of Christ rule in your hearts, since as members of one body you were called to peace. And be thankful."

Since we belong to God, we are set apart. We must be holy as He is holy. We should have Christ-like characteristics inside of us, which are compassion, kindness, humility, gentleness, patience, and forgiveness. No matter how someone treats us, we must do the right thing because we have a relationship with God. We have to account for our actions and every idle word spoken. If we decide to do things in our strength, we can get outside the will of God and eventually fall away from the faith. As a result, we will lose the peace of Christ ruling in our hearts.

Every day, I interact with all kinds of people from various backgrounds. Some are hurting due to the cares of this life, and they need someone to talk to. As a believer, I learned to be friendly and allow God's love to pour out of me unto the lost. I mention God and offer to pray with them. I share that God is faithful. Some people don't want to pray, but most do. If the person's burdens make me heavy, I pray after the conversation so Christ's peace can continue to rule in my heart.

Dear Heavenly Father,

Help me not be swayed by the trials or tactics of the enemy. Strengthen me to share the burdens of others. Enable me to be a spiritual midwife, guiding people closer to you and their purpose. Protect me from burnout and from straying from your will for my life. Instill in me a fervent prayer life. I trust in your faithfulness in answering this prayer in Jesus' name. Amen.

REFLECTION:

How can you encourage yourself not to be weary in your assignment for God?

_____

_____

_____

_____

_____

_____

_____

_____

_____

_____

_____

_____

_____

_____

_____

_____

_____

_____

_____

_____

Day 25

Live At Peace With One Another

1 Thessalonians 5:12-15 says, "Now we ask you, brothers and sisters, to acknowledge those who work hard among you, who care for you in the Lord and who admonish you. Hold them in the highest regard in love because of their work. Live in peace with each other. And we urge you, brothers and sisters, warn those who are idle and disruptive, encourage the disheartened, help the weak, be patient with everyone. Make sure that nobody pays back wrong for wrong, but always strive to do what is good for each other and for everyone else."

Deliverance is the children's bread. When someone is disruptive, unforgiving, bitter, and isolated, they need deliverance. When delivered from various strongholds, we can truly live at peace with one another. We will recognize the enemy operating in someone and combat the power of hell with God's anointing, fasting, and prayer. We need one another, and God stresses the importance of peaceful relationships throughout scripture. God first deals with the church so we can go out into the world and convert unbelievers. Why would they want to get saved when they don't see a change in us?

Social media can bring out the worst in people. Some people post things on their pages that grieve God, such as fight videos, nudity, illicit language, etc. Then, once in a while, they post about God. There is a conflicting message, and that person doesn't have a strong witness. The devil wants to diminish the impact of our witness. People won't take us seriously when we preach a gospel we aren't living. We must get delivered so we don't bleed or spill all our business over social media. When we do this, we can attract the wrong people to our pages who are only coming around to be nosey and to rejoice in our pain or struggles.

Dear Heavenly Father,

I willingly surrender my social media accounts to you. May they be used as a powerful tool for your glory. I am committed to avoiding conflicting messages that stem from double-mindedness. I strive to maintain consistency in my faith journey with you and be a responsible steward of the platforms you entrusted me with. I pledge not to react defensively or retaliate when faced with negativity from others. Instead, I will pray for them and believe in their deliverance. I will not allow my flesh to dictate my actions. I am grateful for your anticipated response to this prayer in the name of Jesus. Amen.

REFLECTION:

What are some steps to follow when dealing with retaliation against you from others? It could be at work, in your family, or in your ministry.

_____

_____

_____

_____

_____

_____

_____

_____

_____

_____

_____

_____

_____

_____

_____
_____
_____
_____
_____
_____
_____
_____
_____
_____
_____
_____
_____
_____
_____
_____
_____
_____
_____
_____
_____
_____
_____
_____
_____
_____
_____
_____

Day 26

May the Lord Give You Peace

2 Thessalonians 3:16 says, "Now may the Lord of peace himself give you peace at all times and in every way. The Lord be with all of you."

The scriptures above are a great prayer that the apostle Paul prayed over the Thessalonian church. Apostle Paul wrote in his letters to the Thessalonian church that the people should have God's peace at all times and in every way as part of his final words. God used him to set order in this church. At times, the church struggled with idolatry, sexual immorality, and faith. Apostle Paul reminded them of God's word and encouraged them to obey it. Imagine how much torment one has when they sin against God. There is no peace. There is a constant waring of the flesh, and the temptation·is at an all-time high. God gives us instructions for a reason so we can live the best life possible without havoc from the enemy.

I wanted to mentor women for many years, but God told me no. At first, I posted on social media that I was launching a mentorship program. I called around twenty people and skimmed the list down to about thirteen. After I called the last person, the Lord said, "I never told you to do that." So, I had to wait for two years to get approval from God to do a mentoring program. God knew that I wasn't mature enough when I wanted to launch out. Throughout mentoring, I have encountered broken people with all types of problems, and I have been able to help them experience God's peace in every circumstance.

Dear Heavenly Father,

Thank you for giving me peace at all times and in all ways. Allow me to give others the same comfort that you have given me. Allow me to be teachable and humble and receive correction from the leadership that you have placed in my life. Fill my mouth with words of edification and wisdom. Allow me to minister and encourage others effectively. Thank you, God, for giving me multiple chances to get things right and opportunities to witness. I love you in Jesus' name. Amen.

REFLECTION:

Write down one encouraging declaration you can post on social media today.

_____

_____

_____

_____

_____

_____

_____

_____

_____

_____

_____

_____

_____

_____

_____

_____

_____

_____

_____

Day 27

Make Every Effort to Live In Peace

Hebrews 12:14 says, "Make every effort to live in peace with everyone and to be holy; without holiness no one will see the Lord."

Hebrews 12 reminds us to be careful how we live. Sometimes, we can become complacent in our walks with Christ and start to compromise. When we begin to feel weak, we must seek God, fast, pray, and read our Bible to get strength. We can fellowship with other believers and listen to faith-filled messages. If we put our guard down, then the enemy will come in because the Bible compares him to a roaring lion trying to devour us (1 Peter 5:8). We must be sober and vigilant and live a clean and holy life.

Without holiness, no one will see the Lord. I can recall a time when I received the revelation of righteousness. I was never the same. I no longer wanted to compromise and knew God's Spirit was with me. My ministry started to shift where people would get healed and delivered every time I preached. I decided to walk in God's peace and not grieve Him by sinning. I cultivated an atmosphere that welcomed His presence so my private relationship could be sensed publicly. What is done in private, God will reward openly.

Dear Heavenly Father,

Help me to shun evil and live uprightly before you. I decree that I will be sober and vigilant. I want to witness the miracles in the Book of Acts in my ministry. I want signs and wonders to follow me. I want to be a vessel for your glory. Help me to have the right motives and do things that are pleasing in your sight. Thank you for answering this prayer in Jesus' name. Amen.

REFLECTION:

How can you remain sober and vigilant against the enemy's plots and schemes?

_____

_____

_____

_____

_____

_____

_____

_____

_____

_____

_____

_____

_____

_____

_____

_____

_____

_____

_____

_____

_____

_____

_____

_____

Day 28

The Wisdom that Comes From Heaven is Peace Loving

James 3:17-18 says, "But the wisdom that comes from heaven is first of all pure; then peace-loving, considerate, submissive, full of mercy and good fruit, impartial and sincere. Peacemakers who sow in peace reap a harvest of righteousness."

God's wisdom is pure, and no ulterior motives are attached. Throughout time, the enemy has given people, like certain celebrities, things with strings attached, such as fame or riches, but the individual will lose their soul in the process. However, when God blesses you, there is no underlying motive because He longs to be good to His people. God's wisdom is peaceful and gentle because He loves and wants the best for us. When we are troubled, His wisdom is there to assist us in a generous amount, and we can ask for it without Him rebuking us.

Years ago, I wrote a book called, *"Wisdom Is The Principle Thing: A Daily Devotional."* I explain how peace and wisdom are connected. We can experience God's peace when we have godly wisdom to make better decisions. We can go to bed at night knowing that we have done the right thing and that God is pleased with our actions. However, without God's wisdom, we won't have peace that surpasses all understanding because there might be doubts about something we should have done or could have done better.

Dear Heavenly Father,

Thank you for giving me keys from your word that help me to discern if something comes from you. I appreciate your loving peace and purity. Thank you for leading me down the straight and narrow path. I will not stray or head down a path of destruction. With you on my side and ordering my steps, I have peace of mind that I am doing the right thing and in your will. Thank you for answering this prayer in Jesus' name. Amen.

REFLECTION:

What are some areas where you need God's wisdom?

_____

_____

_____

_____

_____

_____

_____

_____

_____

_____

_____

_____

_____

_____

_____

_____

_____

_____

_____

_____

_____

_____

_____

Day 29

Cast All Your Cares On Him

1 Peter 5:7 says, "Cast all your anxiety on him because he cares for you."

This scripture reminds us to throw everything at the feet of the cross. When we surrender our burdens at the feet of Jesus, we can experience comfort and peace. When you first go into prayer, you may feel stressed and overwhelmed by everything. However, as you continue into prayer and spend time in God's presence, you will notice a shift where you feel less heavy and more at ease. You will start to feel relief as you get a feeling of peace. God's peace indicates that everything will be okay because He works on your behalf.

During the darkest times in my life, when the pain and hurt ran deeply, I cast my worries on God. He loves us, and when we confess what we feel, He shows Himself to be true to His word. Sometimes, I had no money, but I prayed about it, and God provided. When I was going through demonic attacks against my life and ministry, I prayed about it, and God protected me. In prayer, I received supernatural peace after I let go and allowed God to have His way.

Dear Heavenly Father,

I will not be anxious about anything. You can do the impossible in every circumstance. I will cast my cares at your feet and trust you to fight my battles. My hope lies in you. Thank you for loving me and never giving up on me, even when I didn't do my part. You are faithful even when men are faithless. Thank you for sending the breaker's anointing in my situation in Jesus' name. Amen.

REFLECTION:

What are some areas of your life where you need to surrender to God to have His peace truly?

_____

_____

_____

_____

_____
_____
_____
_____
_____
_____
_____
_____
_____
_____
_____
_____
_____
_____
_____
_____
_____
_____
_____
_____
_____
_____
_____
_____
_____
_____

Day 30

Grace and Peace Be Yours

2 Peter 1:2 says, "Grace and peace be yours in abundance through the knowledge of God and of Jesus our Lord."

Grace and peace are ours. We can name it and claim it. As children of God, we can claim and receive every promise the Lord has for us. We can go to His word, find a scripture, and stand on it. We can thank God daily for it coming to pass as we confess it boldly in faith. When God blesses us, it will be in abundance, so our cups can run over, and others around us can partake in the blessing.

I can recall when I was weary in ministry and wanted to quit. I felt undervalued and not appreciated. The Lord had many women surprise me with scented candles because they knew I loved them. Each woman approached me at the end of one of my conferences with a heartfelt message. That day impacted my life for the next five years. I resisted the urge to quit, and I had so many candles that they lasted for an entire year. I was overwhelmed by God's goodness, peace, and love. He allowed others to pour into me so I could draw strength to keep fighting the good fight of faith.

Dear Heavenly Father,

Thank you for blessing me in abundance. You are a big God, and every giant in my life has to bow down before you. Every mountain has to be cast into the sea. When you bless me, it's beyond anything I can think or imagine. Bless me to receive grace and peace through the knowledge of Christ. Thank you for answering this prayer in Jesus' name. Amen.

REFLECTION:

What are some of your greatest attributes? Think about these things today and praise God for them.

_____

_____

_____

About The Author

Kimberly Moses started off her ministry as Kimberly Hargraves. She is highly sought after as a prophetic voice, intercessor and prolific author. There is no doubt that she has a global mandate on her life to serve the nations of the world by spreading the Gospel of Jesus Christ. She has a quickly expanding worldwide healing and deliverance ministry. Kimberly Moses wears many hats to fulfill the call God has placed on her life as an entrepreneur over several businesses including her own personal brand Rejoice Essentials which promotes the Gospel of Jesus Christ.

She also serves as a life coach and mentor to many women. She is also the loving mother of two wonderful children. She is married to Tron. Kimberly has dedicated her life to the work of ministry and to serve others under the call God has placed over her life. Kimberly currently resides in South Carolina.

She is a very anointed woman of God who signs, miracles and wonders follow. The miraculous and incessant testimonies attributed to her ministry are incalculable, with many reporting physical and mental healing, financial breakthroughs, debt cancellations and other favorable outcomes. She is known across the globe as a servant who truly labors on behalf of God's people through intercession.

She is the author of The Following:

"Overcoming Difficult Life Experiences with Scriptures and Prayers"

"Overcoming Emotions with Prayers"

"Daily Prayers That Bring Changes"

"In Right Standing,"

"Obedience Is Key,"

"Prayers That Break The Yoke Of The Enemy: A Book Of Declarations,"

"Prayers That Demolish Demonic Strongholds: A Book Of Declarations,"

"Work Smarter. Not Harder. A Book Of Declarations For The Workforce,"

"Set The Captives Free: A Book Of Deliverance."

"Pray More Challenge"

"Walk By Faith: A Daily Devotional"

"Empowering The New Me: Fifty Tips To Becoming A Godly Woman"

"School of the Prophets: A Curriculum For Success"

"8 Keys To Accessing The Supernatural"

"Conquering The Mind: A Daily Devotional"

"Enhancing The Prophetic In You"

"The ABCs of The Prophetic: Prophetic Characteristics"

"Wisdom Is The Principal Thing: A Daily Devotional"

"It Cost Me Everything"

"The Making Of A Prophet: Women Walking in Prophetic Destiny"

"The Art of Meditation: A Daily Devotional"

"Warfare Strategies: Biblical Weapons"

"Becoming A Better You"

"I Almost Died"

"The Pastor's Secret: The D.L. Series"

"June Bug The Busy Bee: The Gamer"

"June Bug The Busy Bee: The Bully"

"The Weary Prophet: Providing Practical Steps For Restoration"

"The Insignificant Woman"

"The Foolish Woman: A Daily Devotional"

"June Bug The Busy Bee: Sibling Rivalry"

"All Things Relationships"

"30 Day Pray For Your Spouse Challenge"

"The Christian Drama Queen Mentality"

"30 Days Praying For The Nations"
"Intercessor's Prayer Notebook"
"Prayer Request Notebook Fervent Effectual Prayers Of The Righteous"
"The Prophet's Notebook"
"The Photographer's Assistant"
"The Ultimate Entrepreneur"
"Diabetic Caretaker Blood Sugar Log"
"The Preacher's Handbook"
"Christian Weight Loss Journal"
"Couple's Recipe Meal Planner And Notebook"
"Prophetic Dreams And Visions Journal"
"The Therapist Secret: The D.L. Series"
"Tabuletta"
"Tested, Tried, But I Survived"
"The Wounded Leader: Deliverance And Healing From The Aftermath of Trauma"

You can find more about Kimberly at
www.kimberlyhargraves.com

For Rejoice Essential Magazine, visit
www.rejoiceessential.com

For beauty, hair, and t-shirts, visit
www.rejoicingbeauty.com

Please write a review for my books on Amazon. com

Support this ministry:
Cashapp: $ProphetKimberlyMoses
Paypal.me/remag
Venmo: Kimberly-Moses-19

Follow my YouTube Channels:
Kimberly Moses
Kimberly Finds
The Moses Agency

Index

Q

R

S

www.ingramcontent.com/pod-product-compliance
Lightning Source LLC
Chambersburg PA
CBHW071008120626

46546CB00003B/982